# BAD POETRY NIGHT

# BOOKS BY CLARK

## THE STAINS OF TIME

*The Piano of Death*
*The Boot of Destiny*
*The Chains of Desire*
*The Elixir of Denial*
*The Dance of Dreams*

## OTHER BOOKS

*Those Little Bastards*
*All He Left Behind*
*Missing Mr. Wingfield*
*The Seven Wives of Silver*
*Bad Poetry Night*
*Out of the Woods*
*Under the World*

# BAD POETRY NIGHT

## E. CHRISTOPHER CLARK

© 2018 E. Christopher Clark. All rights reserved.

Published in the United States by Clarkwoods in Chelmsford, Massachusetts.

No part of this book may be reproduced in any form or by any electronic or mechanical means, including information storage and retrieval systems, without permission in writing from the publisher, except by a reviewer, who may quote brief passages in a review. Scanning, uploading, and electronic distribution of this book or the facilitation of such without permission of the publisher is prohibited. Please purchase only authorized electronic editions, and do not participate in or encourage electronic piracy of copyrighted materials. Your support of the author's rights is appreciated.

This is a work of fiction. Names, characters, places, and incidents either are the product of the author's imagination or are used fictitiously, and any resemblance to any actual persons, living or dead, events, or locales is entirely coincidental.

ISBN for the Print Edition: 978-1-952044-04-5
ISBN for the Digital Edition: 978-1-952044-05-2

Library of Congress Control Number: 2018904736

# CONTENTS

| | |
|---|---|
| Frail Words, Frail Deeds | 1 |
| Turn | 3 |
| An Old Danish Goat | 5 |
| It Is Over, Four Leaf Clover | 6 |
| A Penny for Your Penii | 8 |
| We Could Be Heroes | 10 |
| Ain't No Ahab | 12 |
| Missing in Action | 15 |
| The Harbor | 16 |
| Null | 17 |
| Summer Loving | 18 |
| Autumnus | 20 |
| Daddy, Drunk at Christmas | 22 |
| The Blossoming of Ayn Rand | 23 |
| Drunker Than Dickinson | 24 |
| Dude | 26 |
| El Pendejo de Los Angeles | 27 |
| Appetite for Deppstruction | 28 |
| Potty | 29 |
| I Love You Dearest, Dearest | 30 |
| Luck of the Draw | 32 |
| Yellow Swim Trunks on the Lime-Green Grass | 34 |
| Untitled | 35 |
| Supernatural Selection | 36 |
| Parade of the Wooden Soldiers | 37 |
| Little Saint Nick | 38 |
| Sanctity | 39 |
| Gee Whiz, It's Christmas | 40 |
| Accidental Rhyme | 41 |
| All They Do Is Show You've Been to College | 43 |
| Statue | 45 |
| Sonnet 4/28 | 46 |
| Any Other Day | 47 |

| | |
|---|---|
| Debris | 48 |
| Ode | 49 |
| Acknowledgements | 51 |
| About the Author | 53 |

*For all the poets I've taught or worked with over the years, but most especially Richie Hofmann and Jess Rizkallah*

# FRAIL WORDS, FRAIL DEEDS

I only drop a verse
when a story won't come,
when words are a flat pond and
making a sentence
is like carrying water
with my cupped hands
my only vessel.

We are waiting for
the last wave by,
you and I,
but I am no good man,
nor wise, nor wild.
I cry not
for my frail deeds,
in this green bay.

I cry for your stillness instead.
That you do not dance
is what I rage against.

I see you more clearly
than my own memories:
your forlorn face
and far-off gaze,
a crutch to prop
up my imagination.

You are my iceberg,
so much of you beneath the surface
of the water that breaks

around your bare shoulders.

All I need to do is
tell the story
of the twisted strap
of your bathing suit,
of your twisted hair
and the lip you tuck beneath your teeth.

But the author must know more,
my teacher told me,
the poet more still.

I must know
what swims below the surface,
too.

And so, the choice:
to duck my head
into the water,
to hold my breath and
find the truth of you; or to
hold myself up to the mirror
and begin the examination
I am too terrified to fail.

TURN

The bitter boy
beneath the bed,
he was born of a thousand shadows.
The raw material of a man, he is
a puppy with raw meat
in his mouth,
a tongue he bites
because his mother tells him to.

Black blood on his teeth,
and on the knuckles
of the fist he scrapes
against the knots
in the floor, and
in his stomach—

in his ears,
guitars scream
the way he wants to
but can't.
Fingers scrape against strings.
Callouses open
and bleed
like his mother,
who comes
into the room
and brushes two fingers
across his quivering lips,
lips that long to open,
to collude with teeth and tongue.

'Shush, sugar,'
she tells him.
'You'll have your turn
to scream.'

## AN OLD DANISH GOAT

He imagines
his anxiety is a bear trap,
a set of steel jaws clamped tight
around his leg like
grown children still not grown
too old for joy.

But, once upon a time,
somebody told him that
anxiety is a goat.
And that makes sense, too,
to think of it as
a wee hungry beastie
that will eat anything
you feed into its
ravenous maw.

And yet, there is also this to consider:
his mother once said, "Anxiety is
the dizziness of freedom,"
and when he thinks of that
he thinks of when it's the worst,
which is when he's like Grover
trying to nail one page to the next
so that he will not get any closer
to the monster at the end of the book.

## IT IS OVER, FOUR LEAF CLOVER

Don't yell fire in the theater.
Just do your job and
sweep the leaves into the moat,
a bad stew crafted with
painstaking precision.

Lower your voice
when you're cross,
when she crosses you.
When she says,
"I hate your beard,"
when she says,
"Where *did* Dave Chappelle go?,"
lose the attitude.
Order penne with vodka.
Say "I'll have the house dressing,"
but don't say
"there's too much oregano in my marinara,"
even if it's true.

Your love is as
awkward as an aardvark,
misshapen,
a postage stamp, baby,
with no tongue for it.

Or it's violet,
the tongue,
a snack in a tin,
a snippet.

"Do more," she says.
"Rock the casbah!"
Stop, and then begin.
Stop, and then begin.
Laugh your way to pain,
you sore narrator,
when she says,
"You forgot your teeth!"

It is over, four leaf clover.
Count your blessings when she says,
"Please cancel my subscription."
No more Ted Williams,
Jon Bon Jovi,
The Food Network.
No more "We watch *Dazed and Confused* in earnest."
No more "I've never seen *Mean Girls*."

Stop, and then begin.
Stop,
and then begin.

"*Twins* was a decent movie," she says.

*Really?!?*

Don't yell fire in the theater.

## A PENNY FOR YOUR PENII

"Why do I hurt all over?"
he asks me, by way of his puppy dog eyes
and his slobbering tongue.
"Is it the crumbs all over the goddamn carpet
or my assless chaps
or both?"

And the truth is
I don't know.

The only thing I am certain of anymore is that
touching a pug right on
his penis is a slippery slope
that leads to a micropig in
a tiny raincoat and booties chasing
the entire Mormon Tabernacle Choir
into the dreams of Donald J. Trump
on the eve of his second inaugural.
And I'm also certain that, if we ain't careful,
old Donnie Boy will forget to cut the part of
the speech where he goes on about how
life for American Indians was forever
changed when the White Man
introduced them to
road head.

And you know *that* can't come out.
You know they'll have no reservations
about leaving the reservations
and invading this land that
ain't my land, that

ain't your land—
this land that wasn't made for you
*or* me.

So, when he asks me again,
what I tell him is that bit about
what Teach for America is using to
inspire inner city students to succeed:
a snapping turtle biting
the tips of their penises.
And maybe, I say, maybe they've started
doing that to dogs, too.

## WE COULD BE HEROES

Today I yearn to
go back to the drawing board
where I spent summers sketching
heroes that could rescue me
from anything,
maybe even this feeling rooted in my gut,
a nemesis planted there by a vengeful sprite who
sprang from my split skull,
then slithered back inside to have the run of the place.

I am no Zeus, she no Athena,
but still I try to strike her down
with words like thunderbolts.

My daughters hear my curses,
shouted out loud and at myself,
and wonder if the words are meant for them.
Pencil in hand, sketchbook on lap,
I wonder if I can still conjure
the hero they are holding out for. Or,
will they have to rescue themselves?

If they do, I wonder
is that so terrible a fate?
For, isn't our greatest struggle
against the dreams we dreamed of
ourselves that still hang drying on the vine
under Langston's sun?
Isn't every day a confrontation
with the dreams we defer
and defer and defer again,

until they are bombs hurled at us
through time
by the imps we used to be?

Isn't every day a rescue mission
where we are both
the heroine and
the damsel in distress?

And when Peter Parker
pulls on his mask and
disarms assailants with
a joke first and
a punch in the teeth
only after that,
isn't he also
fighting off the tears
of a boy who wasn't
the right kind of strong,
who still isn't,
but might be
someday?

## AIN'T NO AHAB

When at last scroll unfurls
to the place where I find you,
I read the words
"lost overboard"
and I, the barren branch
at the end of the limb
you stretched outward
until you could scratch the scrim
at the edge of the world —
I go overboard, too.

I imagine a leviathan
hungry for wooden ships and wooden boys
come to swallow you whole and drag you down
to the locker of a Monkee
(the one with the tambourine)
who'd made a daydream believer out of me.

When the blue fairy comes,
I wish a fate for you that'd
make Melville swoon,
roll over in his box,
rise from the wooded lawn of Woodlawn,
and take hold of the first thing he might find
to write with.

I want Herman
in a coffee shop
in the Bronx, sipping
something artisanal

as he scribbles down
words that will matter
about someone who matters to me.

But all you've got is right here,
a man with a name no more notable
than it was when you left it to me
(or, rather, to my father, or his father, or
three fathers before he).

All you've got are these fingers,
this set of worn-down keys,
bone-white and battered
as you must have been
when you stumbled into the sea,
leaving the schooner behind
for L'Attila dei pesci e dei pescatori.

Except that there was no terrible dogfish
for you, not even Walt's little Monstro.
You fell asleep at the wheel,
like I did,
driving home with nine inch nails
through each of my eye lids,
only you weren't as lucky.

Then again: maybe neither of us were.
Maybe if there were blood upon the wall I hit
or on the waves you slipped beneath,
maybe then there'd be a tale
the world could marvel at,
the way that we

marvel at a fluke at sunset,

at a whale holding itself high to
say arrivederci.

Maybe.

Maybe.

## MISSING IN ACTION

Flowers held behind my back,
a surprise that you can smell
(even through the reek of
armpits un-deodorized).

The straps of my dress
cling to the two strips of white flesh I've got left
on a body bronzed by sun, not spray.

You hobble toward me,
a crutch clutched under each arm
half a leg taken out from under you.

You grin at
my poor excuse for a bouquet.
I frown at
your smile in progress.

"They're just teeth," you say.
"They can be replaced."

And I know, right then,
I will work as many jobs
as it takes to replace them.

Because you—
there is no replacing
you.

## THE HARBOR

The day the last ship came home,
the widows climbed down from their walks
and served tea and biscuits.

They waited at tables by their windows,
fingers fiddling with doilies,
eyes trained on the dusty lane that led to the harbor,

and they wondered for the last time
whose tables would be empty
and whose would be full.

NULL

Sky sister and the green girl
bleed, baby. And blush.
A hard kiss is how they heal.

These women make warm
the cold universe.
The breeze across
their broken bellies
does not faze them.

Empty, their baskets,
their cartons of eggs
(even when full).
Voids,
vessels
ready to be filled.
Ready, but not eager.
Not waiting.

"Nothing," says the green girl, "is wrong
with nothing."

## SUMMER LOVING

1.
Naked porcelain
perfumed by smoke
on a moist morning.

My corduroys on the concrete,
my coffee poisoned by caramel,
I try to wash away
the salt of sex
and the ocean.

Flies dance through the steam of
a shower paid for by quarters.
You dance back to your tent
through the tall grass,
the dew all you need
to wash yourself clean.

2.
Her fingers ache at
a whiff of honey
from beneath your dress.

Freckles like flecks of
rust on your chest,
your thighs,
the insides
of your elbows.

Once,
when she was a girl,

her brother dared her to
lick the rim
of her tricycle's tire.

She wonders if you might
taste the same,
if you might also
come apart on her tongue.

## AUTUMNUS

Lips linger on
the velvet sex
of a goddess in the grass
who blushes as the last of
her petals sail by on the breeze.

A steel-colored steam
steals across the marble
of a far-off moon that seems to
throb in the night sky
as starlight dances upon it.

I wonder if the goddess can see me
making red-light poetry
of the one moment
of intimacy
she has allowed herself in this season of wither.

I wonder if
she wishes upon me
a brown prairie
in the summer sun,
a river of dust.

The bloom on the vine
that is my wife and me
entwined
came not by the goddess' hand,
but by the machinations of
Hephaestus at his anvil

(or some demigod descendant),
so I wonder if we are safe
from her wrath. I wonder:
could she make our blossom wither
if she wanted to?

## DADDY, DRUNK AT CHRISTMAS

Man's love is like a mystery
you taste in his mustache.

Is it rye, you ask,
or did he spring for scotch?

And is that a whiff of lo mein, or
are you imagining things again,
like him in a restaurant
instead of an alley,
the small space where
he hid from his old man
as a child,
where he hides from the young men now?

The real question is:
why do you holler back
when he hollers,
when he wakes us,
when you know that
this is what he does
every Christmas,
filling that empty
feeling he feels
when he sees
the empty spaces
beneath the tree?

## THE BLOSSOMING OF AYN RAND

An Ayn Rand devotee grows in Brooklyn,
reciting angsty teen poetry when he is not perusing
Anna Karenina's Ashley Madison profile
or reading autoerotic autofiction
written by Atticus Finch before he was racist.

One of the poems reads:
"Balzac's ballsack is
as hard to find as
a good man in a
Bechdel test."

Another goes:
"All happy Brothers are alike;
each unhappy bird pooping on Franzen is
unhappy in its own way."

"Are you there for me, Ayn?"
asks the angsty Brooklyn boy.
"It's me, Alfred.
I've got another one!
It's about a blooming tree as
a metaphor for the female orgasm."

"Ayn?" he says.
"Ayn?"

## DRUNKER THAN DICKINSON

The Lord of emo vampires has convinced
Emily Dickinson to do a keg stand
in exchange for his collected works about
F. Scott Fitzgerald's foot fetish.

And this is not just
a Facebook post from your grandmother
or Faulkner with a mild case of whiskey dick.
This is *The Millions*
describing Zadie Smith's new novel as
"Elizabeth Gilbert's guru and a dystopian heroine
with an anachronistic skill
having a baby."

This is true, baby.
True.

It's me telling you:
having a baby is the anachronistic skill.

So, picture it:
Dickinson inverted,
Whittier and Hawthorne
holding her by the legs while
Emerson holds the tap
to her mouth.

(If you squint, you can see
Alcott in the corner
telling her sisters that
she's got next.)

This is real, man. Real.
As real as
Edgar Allan Poe's mustache.
Maybe more so.

DUDE

    Big bushy operator
    rockin' the vibes,
    his suit,
    some uppers too.

    Athletic chest,
    hardest ode.
    Man of every need.

## EL PENDEJO DE LOS ANGELES

After the earthquake,
Sean Penn brought
elderly Japanese men
to the people of Haiti
because he learned
in L.A. County Jail that
you can trade 200 cigarettes for
Asians who aren't good at math.

## APPETITE FOR DEPPSTRUCTION

"What did Frost eat as he traveled on by?"
Millennials ask, stroking Tolstoy beards.
"What did he eat on the path, on the sly?"

In my mind's eye, a groom and his corpse bride
carry pies and a Sparrow what's been sheared
for Frost to eat as he travels on by.

A choc'latier and a Crane bide their time
till libertine and Mister Wolf appear
to teach Bobby how to eat on the sly.

In July, we eat french fries on french rye
and wait for wi-fi to help us make clear
which Frost did eat as he traveled on by.

"Was it pirate, hatter, or Mortdecai?"
we ask as we career through a career
"*Who* did Frost eat on the path, on the sly?"

"Maybe he was eating Gilbert Grape, guys."
says the prof, and now we all cheer.
"What did Frost eat as he traveled on by?"
Johnny with scissors, in pie, on the sly."

## POTTY

Fuzzy Wuzzy was a bear.
And so, he had some hair down there.

And when he sat upon the loo,
the seat made his poor ass turn blue.

The shit we use to keep it clean,
the lovely scent of the latrine,
it was not meant for beasts like him.
No, we concocted it for Jim,

and Pam, and Stew,
and even you.

But now, we know not what to do,

for Fuzzy Wuzzy was a bear,
was a bear who's now not there.
The chemicals, they killed him dead.
And now, it all falls on our heads.

All because nature did call,
and Fuzzy could not scale the wall;
even a bear wants for privacy.
The privy's for more than you and me.

# I LOVE YOU DEAREST, DEAREST

Here is the church and here is the steeple.
Open the doors and we here—the *People*—
are throwing virgins into volcanos.

For this is the way the world ends.
This is the way the world ends.
*This* is the way the world ends:
not with a bang but with
the penny whistle solo from "My Heart
Will Go On."

The pain is like having anuses for eyes,
or like Miley Cyrus at 55.
It's like a bout with leprosy
at the last glory hole on Earth,
or the heart of a child
pierced by puppy teeth.

It's like waking up half-naked
in a Denny's parking lot
after dreams of tentacle porn and
Daniel Radcliffe's delicious asshole.

This is the way the world ends:
with late-period R.E.M. in concert,
no Bill Berry behind the drums
banging on things like a Muppet
on methadone,
and all of us singing
a dirge about why I can't sleep
at night, about why can't I be you.

I drink to forget
the monkey smoking a cigar made with
the stuff from inside Lance Armstrong's missing testicle,
and with the violation of our most basic human rights.
I get by with a little help from
Judge Judy tap dancing like there's no tomorrow.
But still, I can't help but wonder:
what made our first kiss so awkward?

Was it the centaurs on my tin-plated
lunch box, or was it the Lunchables
inside? Was it my ex-wife standing over my shoulder
in nothing but a shirt from the Boy Scouts of America,
or was it Bill Nye the Science Guy standing over yours?

In a world ravaged by heartwarming orphans
and MechaHitler making the White House the whitest
    house
of all, my only solace is you, my darling, you
and me, and our Five-Dollar Footlongs
and a cup of soup that is still too hot,
that might be forever.

## LUCK OF THE DRAW

You get a five-star Goodreads review
(from your mom) on the novel whose
form rejection slips are fanned out on your desk
like the tail feathers of Flannery O'Connor's peacocks.

At a bar, with the friends you haven't seen since
    your MFA,
you listen to the guy with the TV show
tell the girl you almost slept with that
the next big literary scandal
will pit Hilary Mantel against
a hipster carrying a vintage typewriter
into an artisanal cafe.

You nod.
You almost sleep with the girl again,
then don't.
Instead, she goes home to her spouse
and you go home to yours.

The Sorting Hat put you into
Found Poetry House,
which is where Shelley
would have put Frankenstein's monster,
you swear. Because that's where
every horror belongs
(where they begin also).

The late nights you keep,
the words you write
only with the help of this deck of cards—

you feel like a grumpy dwarf
excreted from a giant worm
into Haruki Murakami's running shoes.

But the words make you laugh
and maybe they will do the same for another,
and maybe that's enough.

## YELLOW SWIM TRUNKS ON THE LIME-GREEN GRASS

    Sometimes he smokes in the kiddie pool,
an ashtray to the side of it.
My grandfather soaks.
His skin, loosening on his aging bones
as his muscles diminish, recede—
his skin kills him.
He scratches till he bleeds
outside, smokes till
he bleeds inside too,
ridding the world of himself
bit by bit.
He wears nothing.

UNTITLED

When I realize
what I'm writing,
I long to go back
through the note
with an eraser and
change the pronouns,
because I don't want it
to be true
either.

I wonder if Kurt looked
at the shotgun
while he wrote,
then I wonder what I might use.
I wield no weapon but these words;
that they are so blunt an instrument
is part of why
I consider the end.

A kiss is the beginning of all things—
two breaths made one make a third.
I wonder then: if a kiss can be
a comma,
a question mark,
or an exclamation point,
who gets to choose
which kind of punctuation
I end with? Me,
or You?

## SUPERNATURAL SELECTION

Pencil hovers above paper
as I decide
which bubble to burst
with a scribble of graphite.

In all my years of failing tests,
never have I ever
wished for an open answer
with multiple choices on the table.

And yet, as I set my pencil down
to keep from drumming it upon your desk,
I can't help but find
the options lacking.

To be or not to be was
Hamlet's question,
but it might as well be
yours too.

For, have my choices ever been
anything but flight or invisibility?
The decision has always been to
stay and hide or to run away.

And what kind of choices are those
anyway?

## PARADE OF THE WOODEN SOLDIERS

Stiff as starch,
the captains march,
and the maids, they are a-winking.

Snow falls down
upon the crown,
for the Lord, he is a-drinking.

On the field,
bands will not yield,
though they are for sure a-stinking.

Overhead,
He's stricken dead
for what He has a-been a-thinking.

Father knows
they'll come to blows.
Their sabers will be a-clinking.

Peace on Earth?
Good will? A dearth.
For the Lord, he is a-missing.

God is dead
'cept in the heads
of the armies still a-fighting.

## LITTLE SAINT NICK

White men in harmony,
the rarest of sights,
and when I hear them singing—well,
you might think I'm crazy,
but I feel like a hot car
on a too-warm winter's day
might heal the world.
I mean,
it's like John said:
war is over,
if you want it.

## SANCTITY

Instead of coal, Santa,
give the bad children
heteronormativity.
Make them understand
the sanctity of a tab
and a slot.

Remind them that marriage can be
nothing but a cheap cardboard toy
you tear out of the box
of your cereal
or your Happy
Meal.

## GEE WHIZ, IT'S CHRISTMAS

Juvenile mind
it's been a long, long time
since you've heard this line
and not thought of the line
for the men's room.

You wonder
what would have happened
if you'd heard this on
the drive home,
the next rest
room a state away.
Would you have peed
your pants
the way the baby did?
And would you blame the laughter?
Would your wife care
about the reason
(or reason)
when she found the piss-soaked jeans
at the bottom of the hamper?

After that,
could you blame her
when he crossed her mind
when she rang his line,
and couldn't explain why
except to say "Gee whiz,
it's Christmas"?

## ACCIDENTAL RHYME

Of all the windows in the world
through which I long to see,
the green one in the concrete is
what brings you back to me.

And maybe I am singing now,
with my accidental rhyme.
A man upon a parapet!
(Is there any other kind?)

Words are a distraction
when feeling's what you seek.
Woman beyond the window,
you whispered that to me.

Your lips brushed 'gainst my ear lobe
my hair caught 'tween your teeth.
"Feel in your bones the hum of me.
Hear not the things I speak."

I tried to turn my ears off,
my tongue, my nose, my eyes—
but they are such very stubborn things.
Oh me, myself, and I.

My mouth against your elbow,
I tried to hum you back to you.
But you frowned and left the bed
that night, because you felt the truth.

I'd heard, I'd seen, I'd tasted,

and oh, how I had smelled.
I'd nosed across the whole of you,
as far as I could tell.

But my weary bones can hold no beauty,
can't even make a fist
to rap upon the window now
so I can tell you this.

## ALL THEY DO IS SHOW YOU'VE BEEN TO COLLEGE

Punctuation painted upon pines,
a forest of question marks and interrobangs;
semicolons, too.
I want to text my English teacher,
tell her, "If it's good enough for graffiti,
it's good enough for me."

But she suckled
at the teat of Vonnegut,
who tells us that the mark
is a transvestite
hermaphrodite,
as if that's a bad thing.

Maybe, *Kurt*,
I'd like to be spooned by
a person in a dress
with half a penis.
Maybe the body comes in
57 varieties,
not just the two that
too many of us see.

Or maybe I'd like to be
in bed with my wife
dreaming of a me
without wrinkles
or folds to get lost in,
instead of here
at this keyboard
trying to decide if or when or

what comes next.

Lincoln said that
for him,
punctuation was
a matter of feeling.
He called the semicolon,
"a useful little chap."

But I'm no president,
no Vonnegut.
There's no Indiana boyhood
in my veins
or in the brains
I wrack now
to find an ending
for this thought that began with
a picture of question marks on trees,
with the question that wakes me
each morning
before the sun has its chance;
maybe a log cabin is
what I need.

STATUE

Chiseled from concrete,
not marble,
she is made of sturdy stuff:
a cathedral of a different kind.

No one stood before
a slab of raw material and
conceived her with his eyes.
Her parents poured the foundation, yes, but
she raised herself
up from there.

So, when you cannot find
the curves you are expecting,
at the corners of her lips,
remember that she is unfinished,
in progress,
under construction,
as we all are.

She will smile
when she is good
and ready.

## SONNET 4/28

Let me not to my love speak words aloud,
nor give my voice to agitations.
My heart is a muted muscle allowed
no sounds aside from its resignation.

Instead, I scratch my weakling's words across
the paper-maker's very cheapest leaf,
like a riddler's chickens skitter across
the frosty road most traveled in my sleep.

And yet, when bare you lay the secrets of
your heart, how do you make them plain to me?
Letters by the hand I have come to love
in the language particular to thee.

My love is no error. This you have proved.
Words written, not spoken, can be just as true.

## ANY OTHER DAY

On any other day, she wouldn't have worn socks.
She would have showered
and spent extra time washing her feet,
cleaning between her toes,
so that all that was left to smell
when he slipped off her boots
was the scent of soft leather lingering.

On any other day,
she would have kept her eyes open,
watched him bury his nose
in the arch of her foot.

She would have kept her eyes open
to watch him close his,
to see him rub his nose against her
until she giggled,
until she said,
"Stop. That tickles."

On any other day,
she thanked God
it was any other day.

## DEBRIS

Pain in the knee robbed me of
a leg to stand on.
Inside, it felt like
pieces of a jigsaw puzzle
pushing against each other
inside a Zip-Lock bag,
trying to get into a groove that was
missing in action somewhere
on my children's floor,
scooped up with
the rest of the refuse
after we waved the white flag
of surrender
and deposited into a Hefty bag
—with dolls' legs
and Easter eggs—
the debris of a privilege
my grandparents bought on clearance,
on layaway
at a K-Mart a long time ago
in a suburb that's never far enough away.

ODE

> There is a language
> scratched upon your pages
> that I cannot read,
> that you translate for me
> with fingers upon keys,
> with knuckles dancing beneath flesh
> worn thin as onion skin
> by the bending sickle's compass
> come to fetch you.
>
> I never learned to read,
> but if you ask me to speak
> the truth for you,
> to sit upon the bench
> where you might have taught me
> to make a joyful noise,
> I would conjure a cacophony
> that would curl your hair
> and the corners of your lips.

# ACKNOWLEDGEMENTS

Many of these poems originally appeared, in slightly different form, on the website Clarkwoods.com.

"It Is Over, Four Leaf Clover" was written in response to a prompt conceived by Nick Ripatrazone for *The Millions*. Writers were tasked with using 35 specific phrases/words from a list, a selection of common words of Nick's choosing, and just 20 wild-card words selected by the writer.

The following poems are remixes of writing from *Cards Against Humanity* and are therefore licensed under a BY-NC-SA 2.00 License: "A Penny for Your Penii," "El Pendejo de Los Angeles," "I Love You Dearest, Dearest," and "Sanctity."

The following poems are remixes of writing from the card game *Papercuts* and are also (just in case, though the makers of *Papercuts* don't specifically request it) licensed under a BY-NC-SA 2.00 License: "The Blossoming of Ayn Rand," "Drunker Than Dickinson," "Appetite for Deppstruction," and "Luck of the Draw."

※

This volume's cover art is based upon the Public Domain work "A Young Man Reading by Candlelight" by Matthias Stom, as photographed by Erik Cornelius for the Nationalmuseum in Stockholm, Sweden.

# ABOUT THE AUTHOR

E. Christopher Clark is the author of the Stains of Time series, a family saga with a hint of magical realism and a whole lot of time travel. His other books include the short story collections *Out of the Woods* and *Under the World*, the novella *The Seven Wives of Silver*, and a collection of poems cheekily titled *Bad Poetry Night*. His short stories have been published in *Live Free or Ride: Tales of the Concord Coach*, *River Muse: Tales of Lowell & the Merrimack Valley*, and the University of Hawaii's *Vice-Versa*. A graduate of Lesley University's MFA in Creative Writing program, he lives in Massachusetts with his wife and daughters.

echristopherclark.com

- facebook.com/eccbooks
- x.com/eccbooks
- instagram.com/eccbooks
- goodreads.com/eccbooks
- pinterest.com/eccbooks
- amazon.com/E.-Christopher-Clark/e/B00H0G94T0